PRE MIDDLE AGE
40 LESSONS IN GROWING THE HELL UP

PRE MIDDLE AGE
40 LESSONS IN GROWING THE HELL UP

COLE HARMONSON

dimmi press

PRE MIDDLE AGE

Published by Dimmi Press

All rights reserved. Except for brief excerpts for review purposes, no part of this book may be reproduced or used in any form without written permission from the publisher.

ISBN 978-0-615-41645-8

Cover Photos: Amy Kaplan Photo
Cover Location Courtesy:
213 Downtown LA, Cole's French Dip

Some names have been changed for the sake of privacy. The publisher and author do not endorse or condone behavior that can be injurious to one's physical, emotional or mental wellbeing, and trust that readers will seek professional counsel when necessary.

Printed in the United States of America

First Edition 2010

10 9 8 7 6 5 4 3 2 1

You think everyone passes by without noticing you. This is for you.

CONTENTS

INTRODUCTION	9
LESSON 1: Don't Hide The Pretty	11
LESSON 2: We Are Afraid, That's Okay	15
LESSON 3: Make Sure You Have A Will	19
LESSON 4: Assumptions Sting	23
LESSON 5: Honor Death As Much As Birth	27
LESSON 6: Embracing The Ma'am	35
LESSON 7: The Benefits Of Stripping	39
LESSON 8: What More Do You Need?	43
LESSON 9: The Power Of The Blanket	47
LESSON 10: Don't Dangle Your Cross In Your Boobs	51
LESSON 11: What Intimidates You Is Next	55
LESSON 12: Angry Driver Is Angry Human	59
LESSON 13: Keep It Short And Sweet	63
LESSON 14: Think On One Thing	67
LESSON 15: Someone You Need	71
LESSON 16: We Need Outlets	77
LESSON 17: There's More To The Story	81
LESSON 18: Dress Not To Embarrass	85
LESSON 19: Flaws Are Good	89
LESSON 20: Sounds Are Symphonies	93

LESSON 21: Wants Are Not Needs	97
LESSON 22: Feel All Your Feelings	101
LESSON 23: Ask First And Share Second	105
LESSON 24: Don't Ask For Pain	109
LESSON 25: Keep Things	113
LESSON 26: Walls Are Good	117
LESSON 27: Set Parrotal Boundaries	121
LESSON 28: Be An Expert At You	125
LESSON 29: It's Clearer Up Here, No Here	129
LESSON 30: You Are Not A Cougar	133
LESSON 31: Handle With Care	137
LESSON 32: Put Up The Canvas	141
LESSON 33: Your Tell Is Your Tell	145
LESSON 34: You Are Part Not The Whole	149
LESSON 35: Learn The Steps To Lead	153
LESSON 36: She Needs It More Than You	157
LESSON 37: Naps Help	161
LESSON 38: Don't Catch People	165
LESSON 39: Your Words Count	169
LESSON 40: It's Here	171
ACKNOWLEDGMENTS	175

INTRODUCTION

People ask my age and rather than saying 38 I want to go ahead and get used to saying it, so I tell them *Almost Forty*. Yes, that's a number.

I need it to be because I'm doing my part to warmly embrace this next decade and all this malarkey about forty being the new thirty is just that. Malarkey. It isn't. It's still forty and I'll sometimes stutter when saying it just like I'll stutter when saying fff…ifty. That'll be okay, too.

In all the fear, if I dig through to the other side, I've only become a better me each year. Imagine if I didn't? Imagine if each year we became more rotten human beings and by 80 absolutely sucked? I'm sure that's the case sometimes but for the most part, for my part, I am desperately trying each year, each day, each moment to be a better me.

I don't want to be the me of my twenties, full of self and self-judgment and judgment of everyone else. I wasn't terribly nice and my ego was through the roof and you couldn't hear the sound of anyone's voice over everything I had to say that didn't amount to much of anything.

And my early thirties. Oh, although I do miss how my eyes looked without the wrinkles I don't miss the way they saw things. Perverted and skewed and unable to see beauty in anything unless it met some image of perfection. Then one day a woman passed by terribly imperfect and I saw everyone turn to stare at her and it dawned on me that all my striving was in absolute vain.

Exhausting.

No, I'll take these years and eyes that are wrinkled from observing and ears that are a bit hard of hearing from finally, finally listening to people. And laugh lines from getting over the seriousness of myself and finding the belly laughter and finding people to belly laugh with. And this almost forty year old body, sure, it needs work but I adore it for seeing me through more suffering and recovering and healing than most people see in a lifetime.

You have me rather excited. Imagine all we'll learn together.

DON'T HIDE THE PRETTY

There's this ridge that deepens along my brow when I'm Cole Angry, which is really Cole Scared, which is really Cole Worried, which is really Cole in need of Puppy Xanax. Where's my Gucci? It generally occurs around April and then my birthday, the holidays and National Donut Day because I never seem to make it to Oh Those Donuts on the holiday and that's just something you're supposed to do. See? Furrowed brow in need of minor cosmetic in-office procedure. I've gone the Botox route and looked, well it must be said, alarming. I think someone saw a picture and drew back in fear. The wrinkle might have been gone and the lines thinned out but Botox makes my face just as mean as a furrowed brow.

The Pretty. The Pretty is important for many reasons. I find great value in seeking it out in lovely boutiques, beautiful museums, great music, interesting people. What I neglected was The Pretty in me. Sure, I can put together an outfit like a pro or design an event for 900 people in mere moments. Give me an Excel spreadsheet and a Droid - I can do anything. But something about that brow and those deep furrows speaks to a place in my heart that stays unprettied for too many reasons.

Hollywood was over the other day. We call him that 'cause he calls everyone Doll and wears a pinky ring and takes early meetings from the East Coast. It was just past my birthday and just past National Donut Day and clearly past April, which is just about the hardest month ever for me since so many really hard things happened in the spring in my life. And he's sitting there and because of the grace of God, I'm laughing and not just laughing but really laughing. Hollywood is not only very Hollywood but terribly funny. He stops, pulls a strand of hair away from my Just Cut Some Bangs Framed Face and says *Huh. You're really pretty when you're not arguing with me.*

He's East and West Coast right. I lose The Pretty sometimes. And it's not something that I can fake because you can see it in that brow that shows all my worries and all my fears and it's the deadest of giveaways. And a little vial of Botox can't hide my concerns because the heart shows what it shows. How good it felt to laugh and to have a face that was light and not worried and concerned-less for a bit and not answering emails and not making decisions and not carrying the weight of this pre middle age world around. It's rather heavy on my pre middle age shoulders. It helps when there's someone to carry some of it for you. Hell, all of it for you. Who am I kidding, to let it all go.

I might just pack it up. Not pack it up as in Hang Myself Pack It Up but pack it up. You know, get out of this place for a bit. Take a road trip and not plan and go somewhere out of Droid Range. Going to work on keeping that brow unfurrowed and keeping The Pretty flowing out of my heart and back into my face. It's there. Sometimes you can't see it, I know, but it is there.

And hoping from deep, deep places that someone will sweep the bangs to the side of my face and say *huh* when they see The Pretty in me.

remember today's fortune:
  to be loved be lovable

don't be an idiot

SOME DAYS, I GO TO THE CARWASH TO HIDE FROM ANSWERING EMAILS.
I STILL ANSWER

DURING THE RINSE CYCLE.

*flowers and gifts and cards and smells
and ribbons and cupcakes just around*

the corner

WE ARE AFRAID. THAT'S OKAY.

I'm afraid of losing my mind and not having anyone to take care of me. I was browsing the aisles of Rogers Gardens Gift Shop looking for a bit of event color inspiration when I overheard, okay, eavesdropped on a conversation. I do that for a living. I plan parties and eavesdrop. A lovely elderly woman dressed head to toe in the safest shades of taupe was talking to her friend dressed in the safest shades of nearly taupe and letting out the biggest fear of her life. She wasn't concerned about her body getting old. It was the mind. She didn't know what she would do if she lost her marbles and no one wanted to take care of an old lady with missing marbles. Marbles are important when you're older. I have one I carry in my purse as a reminder.

It's yellow.

I don't know sometimes how people deal with me and my missing marbles. So I completely get her fear and marbles and them being lost and being older and then adding the burden of having illness and doctor's visits and God forbid the humiliation of having someone else wipe your ass for extended periods of time.

I think one or the other is okay: ass-wiping by someone else or the loss of marbles, but both, both is too much for one person to have to experience. It's like my dad. He has Multiple Sclerosis, which comes with limited mobility some days. Ever wanted to know what it feels like to walk around with cement shoes? Ask someone with MS. In my opinion my dad should never have to suffer from a cold. You should get one or the other – major illness or all the other little random daily sniffles and fevers. Or me. I have epilepsy and sleep seizures that will knock your socks off. I don't think I should also have the flu or a period for that matter. Epilepsy doesn't agree.

Marbles. And them missing. And needing someone to take care of you. Brutal. I had a dream the other night. My dreams are so vivid you could reach out and put them in your pocket. I was elderly and making some soup, which would have to be in a dream because I don't cook. So, I'm making soup and it's my only meal in this dream and you can tell I'm dirt poor, which makes me think I should probably start my 401(k). And all of a sudden I decide to add some seasoning to the soup and stir in ... wait for it ... cat urine. It even has its own special cat urine container. It was feline shaped.

Kill me now. I used to be concerned that I would live my life alone having all my meals at Sizzler, eating cheese toast with my cat. I'm not even a cat fan. Now, it's worse. I'm afraid of lost marbles, including the one yellow one I keep in my bag. And I'm afraid of making soup with no one to share my soup with and for being so looped out of my mind that I would consider cat urine to be a sensible seasoning.

Dear sweet drenched in shades of taupe woman walking around Rogers Gardens Gift Shop with your dear sweet friend and spilling all your fears. I hear you. Even with years to go until I reach your age, I feel your same fears.

I fear with you and for you and I don't know that someone is going to take care of you but I sure hope they do. I hope that there is compassion for the lonely, the poor and especially the marbleless.

   I'm afraid with you. There. I said it.

IT
IS
ENTIRELY
TOO
HARD
TO
DRIVE
WITH
THE
BRAKES
ON.
EVERY
DAY.

MAKE SURE YOU HAVE A WILL

Will Naguib is really Sameh Naguib but goes by Will for one very important reason. His first name was terribly hard to pronounce for some Americans, so he had to come up with his Starbucks Coffee name. When you come from the Middle East, it's not an easy thing always to order a cup of coffee when they insist on putting your name on the cup.

What's your name sir? Sameh, my Will would say patiently, with his best I love America smile on. *Sam? What?* annoyed I-should-be-a-supervisor-but-they-hired-effin-Trevor-instead Starbucks barista asks. *Sameh.* It doesn't take much to raise Will's temperature from hot to steaming. *Sa? What?* Confused, Starbucks barista asks for the last time fearing Will's Middle Eastern temper explosion.

This process could easily go on for hours so Will, my dear Will, using the brain of an MBA, decided to streamline things and create his Starbucks Coffee Name. *It's Will. Thanks, Will. Your coffee will be ready in just a sec.*

Now Will is not satisfied with having a Starbucks Coffee Name; he watched the inauguration and wants to change his last name also. And not just change it but go big and take a presidential last name. We're talking Will Kennedy or Will Washington. He always has erred on the side of patriotism. Wouldn't you? An Egyptian male engineering student who recently got his visa, has a thick accent and has the nerve to fly? You'll know if you run into Will. He'll be the one wearing the Red, White and Beer T-shirt at the airport with a thick silver cross dangling from his neck. Anything to show you he loves America and has no intention of blowing up your plane. Even if Will's engineering brain notices the wing on the plane is falling off and hanging by a thread, don't worry, he won't say a word. He knows if you hear his voice speak up during the flight, he'll spend the night being waterboarded.

So, Will wants to change his last name to something more American, but his real name is Naguib and I love the last name Naguib. When I thought I might marry him, when we were madly in love in the fried chicken, ice cream, beer and flower-in-the-hair days, I loved the idea of walking into Saks Fifth Avenue and being Mrs. Naguib. I thought for sure the sales people would think I was the wife of a rich oil Arab terrorist and they would wait on me hand and foot. There would at least be bottled water.

Mrs. Naguib, would you like something to drink? click clacking in her Saks personal shopper heels hoping I spend enough money so that she makes her fat commission check so she could spend it all. At Saks. *Mrs. Naguib, can I take that to your brand new Mercedes for you?* Yes, I do like the sound of that. That sounds so much better than, *Mrs. Naguib, can I take that to your 1991 Lexus with a dent on both fenders, no air conditioning and no power steering?*

I understand his desire to want to be more Americanized. I get it but I've told him time and time again people will laugh at him. And I don't want people to laugh at my brilliant Will because he wants an American last name and an American Starbucks Coffee Name. I tried to explain to him it's like the ladies in the nail shop that say, Hi, I'm Daisy. And then you look down at their beautician license and it says Thu Nguyen. That's what Will would be doing if he became a Kennedy. He would have better luck being an Obama.

I love Will.

So, he is off to Egypt to visit family and to meet another potential wife, and it kills me every time he goes because I know he needs to fall in love. And, so, I think about him as he's walking in downtown Cairo on the same streets I walked and I know he's eating ice cream because that is his favorite thing to do next to eating $6.99 Chinese buffet for…Three. Straight. Hours. And I'm sure he's found beer because I don't think it's a Muslim holiday or fast, which is just the worst time to travel to Cairo for a guy like Will.

Fall in love, Habibi Kennedy.

arabic i still know

miss you, love you, want you
where's the bar, where's the club,
where's the museum
where's the church

QUESTIONS THAT KEEP ME AWAKE.

WILL MY EYELASHES GROW BACK?
DOES A PRIUS HAVE AN ENGINE?
BEING THE 'ILLEST' IS GOOD, RIGHT?

stay calm in meeti
stay calm in meetin
stay calm in meeting
stay calm in meeting
stay calm in meeting
stay calm in meeting

ASSUMPTIONS STING

Oh, you don't have kids? No? Then you've never been to these places. I was about to lunge across the table and strangle the woman, but her hair was so pretty and straightened and she dressed so nice and she had such a sweet countenance about her.

I didn't think there was ill intent in her question. Just assumptions. They sting. It still makes me raise my shoulder and wince a bit thinking about it.

We were meeting to discuss event planning and children's parties, and she assumed that because I do not have children that I had never stepped foot inside a Chuck E. Cheese, Boomers, girl's tea party or the like. A couple things to note: I'm an event planner. I party for a living. And I used to run a learning center. Boomers, tokens, overpriced stale pizza and field trips to such places? My middle names. My instinct was to rise up and respond with supreme saltiness for assuming that I spent my day drinking martinis in dark lounges letting strange men touch my inner thigh. Hardly the case. I prefer Diet Coke. Instead, I took a breath, looked past her assumption, got through the meeting, walked to my car and wept.

I know, you men and you strong independent women hate to hear me crying but I know how therapeutic it is. I'm crying right now just thinking about crying. Not that I have to validate my tears but tears are valid in this case. Consultants, mothers, dads and all you parents with your babies and all the things you think you know about single people and those of us without children. You don't.

We didn't necessarily plan this. I didn't anyway. I wanted babies and peed on sticks, and even pregnancy tests, every month for years and read every baby book and made my ex-husband insane with all my talk about infertility. I bought the baby clothes and almost bought an Emmaljunga stroller which was the coolest stroller at the time. Almost bought a stroller. With no baby. To no avail. Babyless. So, sitting in meetings with parents is fine, but don't assume we don't know about kids or want them or chose Prada over Pampers. It just wasn't in my deck.

I will not lunge across the table and strangle you. I might go buy a handbag to feel better. I don't have college educations to pay for. Oh, you do?

"PRAY AND VOTE" BUMPER STICKER LADY NEEDS TO "PRAY AND USE B...L...I...N...K...E...R".

HONOR DEATH AS MUCH AS BIRTH

If you haven't already, you should buy stock in Enterprise Rent-A-Car. My poor 1991 Lexus is suffering from multiple organ failure: power steering, oil leakage, no air conditioning and a pissy attitude. I'm going to rent until I find something perfect. I'm the same way with men.

Enterprise it is. And I'm not pitching their product, but that's the one I go to and Wendy is good to me even when I sleep in and forget to bring the car back which happens more often than not. Which was the case last week. I rushed in to drop off the Camry, or was it a Prius…I really don't know. The cars start to blur together. Anyway, I'm waiting at the counter when the woman next to me starts to weep.

Weeping is great in terms of catharsis but sucks when it comes to the reasons why we weep: job loss, broken relationships and then the big one…death. I turned to her and asked because how do you stand next to someone at the counter and see them weeping and not ask what's wrong? It's inhumane not to ask. Intruding is the thing to do.

Her family member has just died and she needs a car to get where they must go and her thoughts are about as jumbled as they should be when death and loss and mourning are involved. I know. I've been to the death place. I've seen the chaos of plans and orchestrating and family and saying the wrong things when what you want to say are the right things.

She is weeping and there is nothing more to say than I'm sorry. So I say it. *I'm sorry. I've been there. It's terrible.* I walk away. She stops me and thanks me for saying…something…anything.

Death is as big as birth and deserves for us not to go silent. Why do we lose our voice all of a sudden when someone dies but can throw a shower when someone is born? Sure, maybe gifts aren't in order. You know? Maybe gifts are in order. This is a time to mark, and I'm not sure where it said we had to ignore the dying or death or the grieving or spend a year not talking to those in mourning until their grief passed. We can be present in grief with them.

My dad and I would often talk about death over breakfast. Don't get morbid; he's not Goth. He's a normal southern man that remembers a time when a funeral procession passing by would cause cars to stop and men to get out, take off their hats and pause in honor of a life lived and lost. I imagine many of these conversations are his heart on the table wondering how people are going remember him. We have these moments over pancakes and eggs over easy, my dad and I. They are over easier to have than at some formal sit down. Diners help. The clang of the plates and the pouring of *too hot and wait a minute before you take a sip of that* coffee helps.

There is something missing in not stopping and taking off our hats. In not stopping our cars. In not honoring a life lived and lost, even at an Enterprise Rent-A-Car counter.

Stopping my car, getting out and thinking of you.

DEAR DAD,
THIS IS YOUR DAUGHTER.
I LOVE YOU MORE THAN CRUSHED ICE.
COLEY

HOSPITALS

I wish there were adult hospitals with music and beautiful art. I'm not talking about fluffy art but art that hurts your guts but not in the way that hurts your guts painfully but in the good way. That kind of way. Sitting outside a hospital that looks like a bunch of cement boxes and remembering sounds and echoes and terrible memories and wishing there was music and art and more laughter and experiences for the people sick and dying and the ones with the sick and dying. How hard would it be to make a place that didn't seem fake but seemed….real.

   I would change to a PPO to go there. You'd be worth the 20%.

POCKETS OF PRETTY

You're never open even though I come to see you all the time and you're never open even though I come to see YOU all the time. Peering in the window and looking at glass in pinks and greens and pretty yellows even though yellows were never pretty and were always thrust upon me in squares mixed with white saying You are neutral and a boy or a girl could be in this room. Glass and bubbles of glass and finally your doors are open for a brief moment and I hold my purse close to me as I roam aisle and aisle and wonder if the closeness of this space will take away my very last breath. Your stairs and your chandeliers and your narrow pathways and soaps and colors beg me to come back and pose with full hair and pretty pale makeup and people to say ooh and then to say ahh but for now I will simply stand in your aisle and take a breath and be thankful you are open to me.

LETTERS

There's nothing to say so for now I write to you in letters that stay far, far tucked away in places that are sealed because who, who, can read a faraway tucked letter? Not me. And in those letters are words and even full sentences that tell dark secrets untold to anyone but to me and – to you. You don't know them though. They are filed to the right and then to the left and only when the time comes for me to say my goodbye when the wrinkles are long indented in my storied face will you read them.

BROKEN CHINA

A piece broke and there's white and blue everywhere and white and blue isn't even my pattern but it's saved in a place that means it's special, was special, to you. So I keep it and nothing is supposed to break and everything is supposed to be kept safe and sealed and wrapped in Saran and then in those special slippery satiny crème covers and then in boxes so that no one can ever get to anything but...

Things break. Things are broken. There's blue and white everywhere and I cannot hide it in Saran any longer and if something else breaks it's going to be okay.

miss cole cole coley
colimanoli coles
duckie nicolia
sweet cole sweet one
doll baby
little girl
baby girl

any girl.

EMBRACING THE MA'AM

Somebody called me ma'am and now I don't know what to do with this dead body. My friend tweeted this the other day and it speaks volumes of my pre middle age angst. You know I have trouble with this four-letter word and I've tried to explain it to you over and over but depending on the camp you're in you'll say one of the following:

Miss Larkin

It's a sign of respect. Miss Larkin is from the South and believes men and women should speak to people like this. In the West we know: It's hate speech.

The Boy

We were sitting at lunch one day in Downtown L.A. and the kind, sweet server made the mistake of calling me ma'am. I swung my head over and furrowed the brow in the non-pretty way I do. *Did you hear what he just said?*

The Boy who is very much a grown-up and more mature than I'll ever be snidely replied, *Well, you are a woman.* Ouch. I did not need him to point out the pre middle age/almost middle-agedness of it all.

Pre Middle Age Women

They, well, you, you agree with me. It starts to happen right around your mid-to-late 30s and doesn't sting the first 50 times you hear it but by age 35 really starts to set in that people might think you are, gasp, an adult. That's the hard part. You're growing up. And although you want to be somebody's baby you're a woman and you pay bills and make decisions and buy things like toilet paper and Italian Vogue.

I want to make this a little easier for you. You'll generally fight the ma'am stage for about three years and then start to give in. It's like a beaten puppy. Oh, a beaten goldfish so I don't piss off PETA. You're like a beaten goldfish. Finally you'll succumb to The Ma'amness.

I rather like the sound of it now.

THE CELLO IN THE MIDST OF A SYMPHONY IS

FASTER THAN XANAX.

THE BENEFITS OF STRIPPING

Beyond irritation this past week. You know when you get to the point where one strand of your own hair makes you kill? That's not a good place. I knew I needed to disengage and go to a quiet place in my head and in my heart.

I went home, which thankfully is very close to my office. Laid down for a bit in my work clothes, set the alarm on the Droid to take a short nap and settled in for some sleep. Kept moving from one side to the other. Irritated. And irritated some more. I got up and took off the work clothes. Laid back down. Still, one side to the other. Couldn't settle into that one spot where everything fades away and it's a very sweet sleep.

It was the lingerie. You'd think I was stripped down enough but I got back up and took that off, too. Crawled back into bed and then…finally….free. Now, I'm not normally a naked sleeper. More the Let The Paramedic Find Me In My Lingerie If I'm Found Dead In The Middle of the Night type. Still for some reason there was a need in my body and in my spirit and in my mind to get to the stripped bare place.

You need that. I need that. Get rid of all that weighs you down, holds you down and keeps you from sleeping sweetly. Remove all the things that prevent you from relaxing and resting and being. It doesn't mean you're going to join a nudist colony or be Naked Guy or Free Girl. Simply realize when you need to unload the heaviness of things and when to clothe them back on you.

No one else knows your irritations more than you and no one can tell what makes you toss or turn more than you. So, take it off, the clothes and the people and the thoughts and the worries and the job and the projects and the pursuits and such.

Stay a little naked for a while until you get some rest. It looks good on you.

NEVER COOK (OKAY, MICROWAVE) NAKED IN THE KITCHEN WITH THE FRONT DOOR UNLOCKED.

WHAT MORE DO YOU NEED?

Fickle Mia is my favorite little six year old and comes running up to me outside our corner market. Her hands wrap around my legs, and I sometimes pretend that her hug for me is stronger than her hug for nearly everyone else. I don't think it really is but I'll imagine so on the days I want it to be.

The first thing we do, Fickle Mia and I, is go inside the market to get ice cream. See, it is Tuesday and her homework is done and she's had dinner so I get to be the one to take her in for a treat. She makes a beeline to the back of the market and opens up the standing freezer, practically sticking her whole body inside deciding between a drumstick and an ice cream sandwich. I'm not sure why we have this same debate every time since every time she gets the drumstick. I still enjoy the hemming and the hawing.

Fickle Mia and I walk up to pay for her ice cream and I remind her to say her thank yous and her pleases and she says them all with grace. We walk outside and peel the wrapping so the chocolate doesn't melt all over her hands. The chocolate melts all over her hands.

And then it happens. I turn for a moment to watch the crowds and in my face is a geranium. A red one. The same type I used to take Mrs. Hackett, my six grade teacher. I would wrap it in foil and Mrs. Hackett would act as if I brought her two dozen roses delivered from the president. No, simply a red geranium sort of tilted to the side and almost a little wilted and one of the red petals is a bit brown but it's in Fickle Mia's hand and her hand is covered in chocolate drumstick drippings.

Could I want another moment more? It's not possible. I have a great list of wants. Diamond studs. Lots of handbags. Consistent electricity in my apartment. Well, that might be it. Maybe a couple other things but when I sit back and think about things like cars and houses and wealth, I am the richest at these moments. Those are the needs in my life. Sweet, little, wilted, beautiful moments. I turned to Fickle Mia and said, *You make me very happy.* She answers full of golden-ringleted curls, *You make me very happy, Cole.* And then she tells me I am 600 and 1 years old.

PAYDAY IS CODE FOR BUY A NEW PIECE OF LINGERIE DAY.

letters written in books warning of hellos
and of goodbyes. i will keep you

THE POWER OF THE BLANKET

It must be said, I love a restaurant with blankets. Sissy, my Rose Colored Glasses Loves From The Belly friend and I went to The Beachcomber Café for breakfast. It was packed, so we ate in the bar. My old church friends would have frowned upon that and perhaps shaken a head or two at me sitting there so early in the morning. The addition of my Baileys might have added to some judgment. I think Jesus is okay with Baileys and beaches and time with Sissy. Sissy had Baileys, too, so in case you are praying for me you can throw her in for good measure.

So, it's beach time and eating time and drinking time and celebrating us time. We finally get a table inside the restaurant which allows us to look less like early morning drunks, which I'm not really minding at this point and Sissy is certainly not minding since she's saying, *We're going to need to stay a bit.* I think the Baileys got to her full of love belly. And she looks over and notices….blankets. Beach blankets. On laps of people. In the restaurant.

I am enamored. With many parts of it. With the idea of being in love and sitting with someone and our little blanket and talking about us and our lives and our work and all things relationship annoying. And I'm enamored with the comfort of it all. I like the warmth of it all.

I remember quite a few years ago, mere moments it seems past my divorce, where it felt like every third second or so I was having an anxiety attack. I sort of wish it felt like sweating and panic but it was this heavy dull pain where I couldn't take a full breath and I pretty much thought I was dying a slow miserable death and wouldn't that be fitting since I was divorced and alone and I better wear that lingerie since the paramedics were going to find me. *Dead divorced but with fabulous hair.* Would that be the headline?

And I would show up at a hospital, they would take my blood pressure, always through the roof, put me in a bed and calm me down with, what I'm sure was an assortment of drugs ending in 'one' or 'ol'. It worked, I realized I wasn't dying and would go back home until the next time I thought I was dying.

And one day, I went into one hospital with the same complaint. Same raised blood pressure. The nurse put me in a room, dimmed the lights, came in and put a warm blanket over me. A blanket sort of like at The Beachcomber. I calmed instantly. And cried instantly.

Somebody took time to care for me.

I think a blanket was all I needed. All you need is for someone to take time to care for you. To put their eye on you and say you are the most important thing to me at this very moment and I'm going to make you a priority and not make anything else a priority.

A blanket says that, especially when it's a warmed one. A blanket at a restaurant reminds me of that. It's a comfort thing and a caring thing and to some maybe it's a keeping warm thing, but to me it's so much bigger. It's being loved on in the simplest way.

Going to get mine out of the dryer right now. So much better when someone puts it on you, isn't it? This will do just fine. For now.

beachcomber   baileys the sissy
beignets more baileys a diet   coke
some sand and people that smile and don't
frown

MY CONVERSATION WITH GOD TONIGHT:
I SUCK AND YOU'RE GREAT SO THAT MAKES US A GOOD TEAM. NIGHT.

to get:
1. *greys*
2. *neutrals*
3. *light stripe cardigan*
4. *crème text/ruff top*
5. *ethnic belt*
6. *tan wedges*

DON'T DANGLE YOUR CROSS IN YOUR BOOBS

Anthropologie shopping the other day. I always look at the center merchandising display first, listen to see if someone greets me even though that doesn't really matter but for some reason I do that here. Then I head to the left for clothes then back to the sale room, try on my tries, head to lotions and then over to kitchen and living and décor.

   Roll your eyes, I don't mind. I love this store and could spend days here. It reminds me of my mom and how I wish she was here for me to take her to lunch and roam here with her for hours. I would love to be The Buyer while she's The Picker Outer. I miss her when I shop here, and it's half the reason I love this place.

So, I'm roaming and find this beautiful salmon-colored blouse that has gorgeous ruffled detailing in the front. I go to try it on and notice there's a small tear. Hating that because I always wonder if they think I'm the tearer just like when you try something on with makeup and wonder if they are going to blame you for the Viva Glam Red. The blouse is still perfect even with the tear and they don't have another large so I'm going to take it. It's closing and there are two people at check out.

Me and this lovely Muslim woman and her son in front of me. She has a large order, a couple thousand dollars. My blouse is on sale for $29.95. She could slide it into her order so easily and her credit card would be none the wiser. No one else realizes my retail logic, so I continue to wait in line.

I watch her while they ring her up. Her scarf is gorgeous and her face is beautiful and I notice this sort of gold medallion in the right lower side of her dress and wonder if there is a matching one of the left side and then wonder if it helps weigh down the dress so it doesn't fly up in the wind. Wanting to ask but not wanting to offend I continue to watch in awe. She's modest and reminds me of the church I used to attend and its traditions of modesty, traditions I didn't used to understand but have now grown to love and respect. I look down at my sweater and tug at the tank underneath ensuring I'm covered. She didn't ask for this but her dress demanded it.

And then I see it. Behind the counter. Anthropologie Girl. She is leaning over putting together Lovely Muslim Woman's order and her boobs are ¾ of the way exposed and as if that weren't enough she has a cross dangling betwixt them. I said betwixt. Yes.

Muslim Woman showed no disgust, nor did her sweet son stare. She had every right to. It was a rather appalling display of breast even for a non-modest woman to observe. No, she was kind and paid for her order and wished Christian Boob Exposed Anthropologie Girl a good day.

I'm all for The Boob. Really. Just sort of thinking hanging the cross in the middle might not be your best sales technique.

I'VE BEEN THROWING EYE EXAMS FOR YEARS TO ENSURE I GET GLASSES. I HAVE A HEADACHE.

- **Accessory** A cardigan, a tote, my droid and my Oliver
- **Actor** Clint Eastwood, Robert Duvall
- **Artist** Joan Mitchell
- **City** Giza
- **Color** More painted walls in faraway places
- **Flower** Peonies, pink ones
- **Guilty Pleasure** Unplanned road trips
- **Hotel** Ritz Carlton after a late night flat tire
- **Ice Cream** Thrifty's Vanilla with my dad
- **Installation** The Umbrellas by Christo
- **Jewelry** My grandfather's WWII ring
- **Magazine** Monocle
- **Memory** Designing a catering menu with my mother
- **Museum** The Museum of Contemporary Art, Los Angeles
- **Perfume/Cologne** Hanae Mori's Butterfly with a touch of Creed Santal on top
- **Singer** Melody Gardot
- **Time of Day** The late hour
- **Person** The lonely

falling the cable was strong

WHAT INTIMIDATES YOU IS NEXT

Last week's rental car was a Prius. Don't tell anyone, but it scared the hell out of me. I tweeted help requests asking where the cigarette lighter was. I know, I know…none of you Prius owners smoke or if you do, you smoke green, organic cigarettes that are grown on green farms and all the workers that till the tobacco leaves sit around a table at the end of the night breaking bread together, writing poetry and sharing stories of how to make the world better. Those kind of cigarettes and that kind of smoking and those kind of Prius drivers. I'm just looking for the outlet so I can plug in my phone.

And I find it after getting a text from The Boy because he doesn't always respond, but when there is a need he watches my tweets and answers the call to action. He's sort of Batman-like. My tweets are a batcall.

The Prius scares me. It still does. It took two weeks of rentals before I figured out you needed to put your foot on the brake to get the engine to start. Still, I like this car, this car that terrifies me. Something about conquering something I don't know anything about and am a little afraid of turns me on. Great, now I'm going to have to conquer planes. They terrify me right now, too. Only the ones with engines.

The Prius. It's a really cool car and great on gas mileage, well, when you learn how to start it. And it zips in and out of parking spots really easily so the chance of me crashing into cement posts or other cars or people is highly unlikely. Retract – is less likely.

It's a great car. It only took one week for me to learn how to use the shift and now I am a Prius Master and have decided to offer classes. Colored belts will be issued at different levels of mastery. See me for details after I learn how to turn off the windshield wipers.

IT GRIEVES ME TO SEE FOUR CARS
PARKED OUTSIDE A MUSEUM.

ANGRY DRIVER IS ANGRY HUMAN

It was a very innocent left turn into what could be said was mass amounts of oncoming traffic in the middle of the busiest time of the busiest street in Newport Beach. I should know by now not to mess with Orange County women either picking up their children from school or racing to the next boutique for those precious little matchboxes that have those little designs and you don't really want to use them but do really want to display them in jars.

It can be a beast to cross traffic when a woman is on the hunt for the perfect matchbox for her next dinner party. I was the victim of such traffic. And it was just a left turn really not even a full street crossing with intent to go to a bakery and get a croissant or anything full of malice like that. A left. That's all and a tiny one at that. I inched my way halfway across the road and hovered in the middle lane. What do you call it? Sort of that Double Dotted

Line Turn Either Direction lane. Ugh. You men know the one I'm talking about.

And she did it. She not only honked her horn at me as if I was about to steal her child. She laid on it. For a while and gave me a salty look, and then when she passed me she looked back and kept up the saltiness for good measure. It was rather smooth, and if I had a hat I would tip it to her. You have to admire a woman with that much grrr in her heart, but it was not even a full left and I didn't mean to cause her any harm and my rented Camry, or was it the Prius, was not even really in her way.

She wanted to honk. She had the honk in her. She saw the ass of my car in the distance and got her honking hand ready. I could venture a guess and say that hand stays prepped to honk most of the time she drives. I'd also put a good twenty on it that she has a hot little temper to match the quick hand to the horn.

Angry driver is angry human and how you drive is how you are. You can tell me the drive is different than the driver, but I haven't seen it to be. Nope, not in these pre middle age years. I've been you. I'm the master of the angry response, having flashed my lights and rode a car far too close for comfort and laid on a horn or two in my younger days.

And then it hit me. It was starting to look a little foolish when I'd throw my fit and we'd end up at the same light together. Humiliation tends to work really well at fixing my hot toddler-like attitude.

Angry driver is angry human, and I'm not there yet. No. I still have The Angry in me and that one strand of hair gets wrapped around me sometimes and makes me want to scream and the furrowed brow gets way too furrowed but I'm wanting, I'm craving, I'm desperate to be calmer and kinder and gentler and more graceful and to use the horn for more important things like......

Can I get back to you on that?

WILL FINALLY PHONED.

ME: I COULD HAVE SLIT MY THROAT FOR ALL YOU KNOW.
WILL: YOU'RE TOO VAIN. IT'S A VISIBLE SCAR. HOW
ARE YOU, HABIBTI?

KEEP IT SHORT AND SWEET

Damian is a friend of mine from high school who even way back then knew all the big words. I knew them, too. We were in Academic Decathlon together and sure, he was better at math and science and I chose D when I didn't know the answer to something which was more often than not. Still, when it came to the Super Quiz I kicked everyone's ass and that's what really counts, right? At UCLA while I was camped out protesting in the quad, Damian was studying. He became a successful attorney. I pick out sexy lounge furniture and cool bar drinks for a living. Huh.

The big words. I still know them but I don't like using them. I like the small words. I find them accessible to more people and the big words scare people sometimes and other people pretend they know them but then rush to their phones to look them up or other people don't rush to their phones to check them and use them in the wrong way. And then there are the people that love big words just for the sake of them being big. Those people get under my skin. I think there's a bit of an intimidation factor there, sort of like LBJ grabbing the balls of his staff. I appreciate the approach and I know it gets things done but don't do it to me or to people I know.

Big words. And small words. And words people understand and words people think they understand and then the words they do. See, that's why I love children's books so much. There's such a deep simplicity to them and if you don't have a collection of children's books on your adult bookshelf you are missing out, Kiddo.

They are the best. There is a book by Cooper Edens, If You're Afraid of the Dark, Remember The Night Rainbow. It is full of simple, sage advice and the most beautiful illustrations. Sure, you can read Siddhartha again or go climb a hill and ask a snake what direction to take your life, but occasionally, on those days when you have to keep your career afloat and all the balls juggling so terrifically in the air, a children's book is the perfect anecdote to crawling under your desk to shake uncontrollably. Do you need more sound advice than, *If you find your socks don't match stand in a flower bed?* I think not.

SAT DOWN WITH STYLIST BEFORE EVENT AND TOLD HER I
WANTED MY HAIR FLAWED.

st pride ambition
l   fear

jealousy
impatience
selfishness
ess
ess
LIKE ME.

THINK ON ONE THING

Lisa was with a client when I walked into Happy Nails tonight so Terry took me into the back for my wax job. *What are we doing today, Cole? Get it all. The brows, lip.* I'm not sure what side of the family gave me all this hair but so grateful it's almost blonde and at least doesn't scare people the way that lady at the one store does when I see her arms. It's like a coat.

She finishes and walks me outside and I feel like my face is bleeding and stinging and I suppose feeling pain is better than threading because I want to stab my eyes out each time Terry threads me even though she talks me into it every single time. Wax? Done. On to waiting for Lisa because going to someone else would make Lisa very, very mad. I try not to make people mad that have access to sharp instruments and my flesh.

Lisa is taking her sweet time because she knows she's in high demand and Terry comes over and asks if I want a massage. I'm in a yes mood. Sure. I take off my sweater and remember to put down my phone which rarely comes out of my hands. Okay, the phone is away. The magazines are down. I'm going to relax and enjoy this.

Wanna hear my version of relaxing? Welcome to my brain:

I hope the oil doesn't stain my new sweater. Not going to put that on until I wash this oil off. Wonder if Lisa is almost done? Does she have the color? God that feels good. Why hasn't he called? Don't check the phone. Don't check the phone. Have to get tickets for this weekend. Hollywood still hasn't texted me back. Wonder if he's going to be around this week. She's touching my eyeballs. I need my eyeballs. She's going to poke out my eyeballs. That feels so good on my eyeballs. Will you please go back to my shoulders? I don't need my eyeballs rubbed. You said you're touching my pressure points but those are not even distance apart. Now those aren't either. I wonder if I do have ADD. Wonder if getting the Droid caused it or if I always had it. So want the rest of that Croque Monsieur for dinner. Five more minutes? Sure. You're completely messing up my hair and that guy is sitting right there and I know he is looking at me which is so obnoxious of me but I know he is and my hair is a mess and now my makeup is completely screwed up but whatever what am I going to do at this point. That feels really good. Why didn't I enjoy this? Really want to go see Kyle in the desert. He gives the best massage and then maybe I'll only stay for the day and go shopping afterward but it will be worth the money to pay to go see him. Yah, because he'll make me cry and ask me what's wrong and I'll tell him I feel like people dump me in the trash can.

Your 20 minutes are up, Cole. Did you enjoy that? I did. I would have. I sort of did. I would have more if I could learn the art of thinking on one thing. The other day I had a dream, another one of those really real ones, the type I can touch and hold and taste and feel and talk to. And in it, I saw and felt and experienced the phrase: Think on one thing. It is the thing I need to do and the thing I need not to do is to think on many things. My brain is wired naturally to be all over the place in a very creative way and you, dear one, have the same brain. You read and you love and you live and you think and you want and you dream and you desire and you build businesses and then they succeed and then sometimes they fail and then you have more dreams and then you put your dreams in your pocket for a bit. It's an active brain. I challenge you and me and you again and me three times over to: Think on one thing.

It takes effort. You wouldn't think so, would you? One thing would seem like the easy thing to do but it's harder to think on one thing than a million things. It's the adult thing, the pre middle age almost middle age almost completely mature thing to do to stop and focus and pick the most important moment to have and, well, have it.

Maybe it's eating an ice cream with Fickle Mia or watching her stick a red geranium in your face. Just have it and stay there instead of somewhere else. Tomorrow has enough worries or so I've been told.

I SEE HUGE FIREWORKS AND IMAGINE THEY ARE ESPECIALLY FOR ME. IT'S OKAY BECAUSE FICKLE MIA WALKS INTO THE MARKET HULA-HOOPING

BUT THERE'S NO HOOP.

SOMEONE YOU NEED

We need things, us pre middle agers. Think about it sort of like your own diaper bag stocked full of wipies and Cheerios and binkies but instead you'll need, well, a couple different things. Oh, you can keep the binkie, but I'd soak it in whiskey. And the wipies might come in handy for the drool running out of your mouth from one of those real tired sleeps. And, yah, keep the Cheerios. You don't have time to get to the market anyway.

Someone to push you off cliffs.

Come on. I'm not talking about a real cliff. You're at the age where life gets stressful enough and if you're going to do that, well, you're going to do that. I hope you don't do that. It's a rocky fall and a bloody mess and the press comes and it's a whole thing.

I'm talking about when you are stuck in the place of indecision between *should I try this business or stay in my job that makes me hate my life every morning I wake up.* That place of indecision. Miss Larkin is my entrepreneur friend and believes in the power of developing your own business and being creative and dreaming big dreams. And pre middle age is the time when we normally sit on the edge of the cliff debating jumping off and trying big ideas or we inch away in fear.

That's when you need a Miss Larkin. You need someone to push you just hard enough to see that the cliff isn't really so steep and the dreams are completely reachable and chances are worth taking and if, if, if you screw up so bad that your pre middle age business fails, well, you can try again in middle age. You are still young, friend. You have many, many years in front of you to make a complete and utter success out of things. So, find your someone that tips you off cliffs and keep them in your pocket. You'll need them in these years.

Someone with rose-colored glasses.

Her name is Sissy, that's what I call her anyway. She might as well wear the glasses all day long because on any given day and in any given circumstance she will see the brightness and the lightness and the right in a situation.

You'll need that in your journey.

You know why? Things are going to get a little dark and dreary and you might find yourself in a corner crying and tearing at your clothes. Oh, that was me. Well, maybe that is you, too. And you men, you tend to throw your fists into drywall when you are losing it. This is the time when someone like Sissy comes in handy. She sees the best in your worst and she sees through to the other side of your dark tunnel.

Your glasses are a little foggy and they look sort of smudgy. You haven't cleaned them against your shirt lately, have you? Sissy will take care of that for you.

Someone that dances.

Miss Stacia Rae will find any excuse to dance, and it normally happens at the most inopportune times. We were at an Angel game, which absolute pains me, being a Dodger fan. She gets a call from her mom. Turns out her brother is on the other side of the stadium, which clearly means this woman, this pre middle age woman will spend the rest of the evening dancing and acrobatting to ensure her brother a million miles across the field spots her.

There is a physical ease to this woman that my body needs in all its tension. And I used to be so prim and proper about things and try to calm her and her kinesthetic expression down. I looked at her in that blue and yellow Linus-striped sweater in all her gangliness that really isn't gangly, but is a model in hiding, and laughed.

She is exactly what I need every day of the week. She oozes ease and makes my body calm with her outbursts of energy. I watched her jump in the air and wave her hands inning after inning after inning until finally, in the bottom of the eighth, her brother spotted her. I think it may be the same way with her and love. Cannot wait to watch that inning, too.

Someone with her head on straight.

I call her Red since she lives in Canada. I'm trying to accept it and embrace her leaving the country. It's our own personal North American Free Trade Agreement, I presume. We give you Ally for a while, and you can host the Winter Olympics.

Don't live your life without a Red. Pack her up in your pre middle age bag and don't let her go. She's vital to your operation. When you feel like you are headed to Crazy Land, phone Red on the red phone and she'll calm you right down. She probably will be making dinner, making out with her hot husband and drawing creatively with her brilliant child at the same time, but she'll calm you right down.

Red pays her bills on time. She saves for the future. She makes doctor's appointments. And keeps them. She charts things. She cooks things. She makes trips to places and take pictures and on top of it buys and wears sexy lingerie. Just not on Sundays. Red's got her act together. She'll never boast about any of it though. I think she's almost done solving the conflict in the West Bank.

ONLY
LISTEN
TO
MUSIC
YOU
FEEL
IN
YOUR
GUTS.

WE NEED OUTLETS

I was supposed to go to this get-together that didn't come together, and as an event planner that makes absolutely no sense to me. Rather than acting like Cup Half Empty Girl I cooled my jets and went to a museum because a museum is the place I go when things either don't make sense and I need them to or when I am pissy as hell.

I was pissy as hell.

It worked and got the creative juices flowing enough for me to feel brain steadied and seeing colors and light and textures and movement was good. There was this one piece that was full of brilliant fuschias and salmons and charcoals and blacks against a white background, sort of an abstract expressionist piece and at the bottom there was an exhaust pipe.

Exhaust coming out of a piece of art. I like that.

In art and in life I like that. I looked at my Prius the other day and wondered rather aloud why the car had an exhaust if it runs on a Duracell. I'm not quite sure if it really is a Duracell or a large solar panel on the top of the car like my parents had added to the roof of the house to get that discount from Edison. You know, one of those Green things that I should know more about and don't. Either way, what is an exhaust doing on a Prius, and then someone is kind enough to tell me that there is still an engine in the car. Which in some way I guess I knew but the thing is so stealth and you could completely commit a murder in it 'cause it is so quiet that I really wasn't sure about the engine part of the car.

I guess now the exhaust makes sense.

So art needs an exhaust and a Prius needs an exhaust which means all other cars do, too. Huh. I finished at the museum and walked over to have lunch at Daily Grill. This sweet mother and her young son were walking past me. He looked quiet and pensive and lost in that little boy thought that makes you wonder what battle he is fighting or winning or what city he might be building. And out of nowhere he shouts from his sweet pensive little boy mouth *Ninja!* and keeps walking.

We all went on. Me to my lunch. Mom and the boy about their day. It made perfect sense to me. He had an exhaust valve and needed to let out some words. I get it. I wish I could sum up all the thoughts in my head with a Ninja phrase and keep on going with the ease of this little one or paint a picture with the beauty of that artist and have the exhaust coming out the bottom of the art. Or maybe even be a car that knew when to take things in and when to let them out.

It's harder for me. I keep in too many of the words I need to let out. And then I let out too many of the words I need to keep in. My exhaust is a little twisted. I'm going to work on that. I want to learn how to say what needs to be said in the right manner and not say it in the wrong manner.

Maybe I'll walk around random places and yell out *I'm scared* or *I'm tired* or *I'm worth loving* or *Please hold the door for me because I'm a human, too.*

Cole's Top 12 Lessons of 2008

12. You can live for 12 days without electricity. Drying your hair in the car works. Comes out rather nice.
11. Epilepsy is, well, fourth of July with the fireworks but no parades or hotdogs or Cub Scout troops walking by with banners.
10. Fall, get up, dust off, cowboy up and don't settle for anything less than the za za zu.
9. It's possible to enjoy a good meal alone and be a woman. And you don't have to pretend to read the paper.
8. If kissing someone doesn't feel like an epic war novel then don't marry them. It'll be epic and it'll be war but it won't be a very good novel.
7. Always go with your gut. Not their gut, your gut, because when they leave they'll leave your party.
6. A good solid deli is a place to make decisions.
5. Do not waste another decade not liking your arse or your legs or your face or your belly. Cause they do.
4. Engaging is more important than being engaged. Loving matters more than being loved. Giving blesses more than getting and getting.
3. You will not die if you spend a day alone.
2. Living without cable is quieting, not deafening.
1. More than anything I awaken and still want more of God and less of the mess that is me.

I went back to the museum tonight for a film screening of Jean-Michel Basquiat: The Radiant Child and walked by that piece again, the one with the exhaust. A group of three were standing in front of it, deciding what that piece dangling from the bottom was. Clearly to me, it was, and is an exhaust. Clearly to the post middle aged woman who apparently is having a rough go of things with her lover, *it's a flaccid penis.*

We need our outlets. We do.

TEARS AREN'T ALWAYS SAD.
SOMETIMES THEY ARE FRIDAY.

i could use a mom these days.

THERE'S MORE TO THE STORY

Lisa was finishing my nails and they looked so pretty and she complained in the very immodest way she complains that I need to come see her more often because *don't your feet look better now that I take care of them.*

They do, Lisa. I love you.

I'm reading my magazine and trying to focus on relaxing and feeling super guilty because the shop has closed and I asked her not to paint my toes and said I would come back another day. She insisted I stay and said she normally stays late. That didn't make it all right but I kept reading and choosing who wore which dress better.

I didn't really care. I don't like competition between women.

Her phone rings, Lisa's that is, one of the last remaining people I know that has a ring tone other than an old fashioned ring. She picks it up talks for a few minutes, hangs up and smiles. *It's my son. He told me to bring home milk.*

A million thoughts run through my head that is supposed to be thinking on one thing. I miss my mom. I remember calling her when she was late coming home from work and reading off the list of things I wanted and now being an adult and wondering how tired she must have been. The thought of one more stop must have been just too much some days. I feel awful for keeping this woman here when her son wants to spend time with his mom and could probably care less about the milk but cares much about seeing her.

The last thing I want right now is to have her painting my toenails because all of a sudden she is not my nail lady, she's a woman and a mother and someone that gets tired and has long days and loves and probably has a man that loves her and makes love to her. And I look at her more as she continues to paint and notice her makeup and how beautifully it's done with such detail and I can imagine her home is the same way. Detailed and refined and she's not just some woman that puts my feet in a bath of water and gives me a foot massage and makes this amazing custom color for me every time she does my toes. She has a family and a story and she's a human being.

It makes me ill in a heart way.

Her name is Lisa. If you see her, do say hi. And if you happen to be by the store, pick up a gallon of milk for her, would you? She needs to get home to her son.

EXPECT IF I STUFF MY CHEEKS WITH ENOUGH
SOURDOUGH, I'LL BEGIN TO FEEL BETTER.

DRESS NOT TO EMBARRASS

I had to make a quick run to Target yesterday and was letting the walkers pass before me. I like to watch people and it was definitely a people-watching sort of day. There was the dad clenching tight his little boy's hand as they crossed and the elderly couple taking their sweet time, which they are allowed to do since they earned it, and then her. Tank Top Woman. She's in her 40s and her skin is tanned and ready to be skinned and used for a seat cushion. Very pleathery. Nice if you like that sort of thing. I don't mind your decision to kill off early with tanning. It leaves more parking spots for the rest of us.

It's the tank top and not really the tank top itself because that would be fine but your insistence on letting the right strap dangle off your shoulder as if you were a coquettish 15 year old calling in the boys.

You're not, Sweet Thing. You're in These Years and you need to pull that strap up. It's not cute anymore. It looks a little inappropriate (whorish). You seem in need of attention (desperate).

Pull it up. It's time to act your ma'am age with the rest of us. I gave in, too. Pulled those straps right up and started wearing adult clothes which can still look cool but in an adult way not in a *I Hope to God Someone Thinks I Am 23* Way.

That's not bringing The Pretty.

IT'S
ONLY
LOUD
IF YOU DON'T LIKE IT.

pay cell
ll will — today,
eeting at 10am

FLAWS ARE GOOD

I get more compliments on this ring than on any other piece of jewelry I've ever owned. Believe me, it's not that precious. Well, it's precious to me but it wouldn't be precious to you and if it fell on the ground and you grabbed it and didn't give it back, which would be absolutely brutish of you, but if you did that and kept it and went to get it appraised you would come up right around $250.

Maybe a little less.

And then there are the two missing diamonds, in fact, diamond specks, let's be honest and call them what they really are, diamond bits that fell out recently. Every time I go to get them replaced, another one or two falls out. I've given up replacing them and come to accept the truth that glares me in the face daily.

My ring is flawed like I am flawed and has things missing from it like I have things missing from me and, even though it's shiny like I am shiny, it still isn't perfect.

That's what is pretty perfect about it. And you, you are so drawn to my flawed ring. Some of you ask if it's from Tiffany and Co., and me, being all things non-fiction, blurt out *No!* And then you gaze at it wondering where I got such a ring and don't realize the smallness of it and the littleness of the cost of it. And I tell you and I point out the missing diamond bits and show you what should be so obvious.

It's flawed like me.

You still like it. You still like me. I suppose I could search for another ring, yes, I've browsed those stores and mulled the thought of getting something shinier and sturdier, but this is honest and chipped and bruised and it's been through some things and had a tough go and still is hanging on and not really even just hanging on but thriving and sort of really brilliant and shiny and diamond-like. Well, because it is full of diamonds. Real ones.

Sweet Darling Girl and you, you Precious Man, you don't have to hide your flaws. I like the imperfect perfectness or perfect imperfectness of them all. So shiny.

THE THING WITH ROAD TRIPS IS EVERY TIME I TURN BACK

I'M TOO CURIOUS ABOUT WHAT'S AHEAD.

SOUNDS ARE SYMPHONIES

Around 6ish every morning the cars start going down the street this way and down the street the other way and there is a zizzing and a zazzing to the road that reminds me of Cairo before prayer.

I like remembering early mornings alone in my tiny hotel room at Hor Moheb waiting for the day to start and awaiting the call to turn to God. The cars told me that was coming and now, in my downtown, they tell me the day is starting.

I welcome it in the groggiest way I can with one eye open and check my emails and all the event fires that beg my attention and answering so early. And then, roll over to the side that hasn't been slept and rest and listen and think. The cars continue to zizz and then they zazz. And sometimes they honk in that angry laying on of the horn way when someone wants to go through a light that is almost not green as if there will never be another one. Ever.

Some of you are bothered by the zizz and the zazz of the morning and prefer earplugs that cover all those sounds. You want nothing of the morning music I so desperately love. It's a symphony. Lawns being cut and doors opening and coffee pouring into cups and alarms going off in our personalized way. People yelling in their morning yells with reminders to *pick up this and grab that and not to forget those papers over there on that table.*

I love my symphony. When you are tuning you get a bit under my skin. It takes you time to warm up, you morning sounds but once, yes, once you are working together and all are in harmony I drift back off to sleep in an orchestrated rest.

You have my applause for today's performance.

CHRISTIANS REALLY SUCK SOMETIMES.
I AM ONE. SORRY.

WANTS ARE NOT NEEDS

Electric companies. When they send you a bill they want payment. And when you ignore that bill, they send you another. And when you ignore the late payment bill, they send you another, but this time they put Please Respond Within 48 HOURS on it. In red.

And when you ignore that one, you get another letter that says you are scheduled for immediate disconnection. It's the adult version of "If You Give a Mouse a Cookie."

Walking through the front door becomes a game of chance. There's this pause that happens where you feel about a three-second delay while you wait for the light to kick on. Most of the time, it does. Most of the time.

I'm flipping the switch daily to see when that electric company is going to flip the switch on me. It happens on a Tuesday. Grrr. Should've set some candles out. Should've found a way to pay the bill. And, I walk to the counter, set my keys down, put my purse on the barstool, walk over to the French doors, open them up to get a bit of light inside, find my leather chair and just....sit. It's quiet. Dark, yes, but quiet. And sounds so peaceful.

Time for a powerless candlelit shower. Sexy, huh? You're getting a little turned on, aren't you? When on earth would you make time for a candlelit shower on just your average Tuesday? I had the pleasure of doing this six nights in a row thanks to my empty wallet and drained bank account. Not so sexy, huh? You're less and less turned on, aren't you?

I can quickly distinguish between a want and a need. Power isn't really a need for a single girl living in warm weather. It feels like a need, but it isn't. It feels like water and air, but it isn't.

On the end of the sixth day, the flip was switched. I had power again. And, the flip was switched. I had a much clearer understanding about what I could and couldn't live with and without. Sometimes, being in the dark will do that to you.

Checked my mail today. I have another one of those red notices. This one says Please Open Immediately. I'll look at it tomorrow.

I LEANED OVER TO PLUG IN MY LAPTOP LAST NIGHT.
GOT MY HEAD WEDGED BETWEEN THE CHAIR AND WALL.
FOR THREE MINUTES.
DEBATING BETWEEN STARTING YOGA

OR MOVING THE CHAIR.

FEEL ALL YOUR FEELINGS

My feelings have a tummy ache right now. I'm feeling this real big invisibleness from multiple fronts. If I had a superpower you would not be able to see me. My weakness would be Gucci or m&m's.

Lichtenstein has this piece where a woman is shouting out, "Hello?" I'm not a huge Lichtenstein fan with his black and white dots that make me feel seizurey in the middle of crowds. This piece grabbed me though. She was feeling invisible to someone, maybe to many someones the same way I was feeling superpower invisible to everyone even though I didn't want to have that superpower. I would have much preferred to have to ability to see into the future but that destroys my whole needing to have faith without seeing deal. Note to self - decide which superpower to ask for before next meeting.

Hello? Do you see me? You, sir, saw me carrying two large buckets and a bag and walked into the store and closed the door on me when you could have held it open. Aren't I someone to hold a door open for? Isn't everyone someone to hold a door open for?

Hello? Do you see me? Family and friends. I'm drowning and walking around like a zombie with my fake smiling event planner face on pretending like everything is fine but it's not fine at all. The only words coming out of my mouth and into my head are, *I don't want to live.* And I know that's not something I'm supposed to be thinking but they are my thoughts and I'm having them and this would be a time I'd really like you to answer when I say

Hello? Do you see me? I'm working as creatively as possible and you want more and more and I'm out of juice and if you send one more email I'm going to walk into the ocean and swallow water.

I have no more smiles and you need me to have smiles but my superpowers are running out. I'm invisible, sure, but not in a powerful way, in a terribly terrible way. I need someone to see me. My feelings have a tummy ache. I probably need a warm beach blanket. I'd like someone to say I have my eye on you.

I'm feeling all my feelings. My tendency was to ignore them or donut them away but I've decided to feel them. It's painful. It requires lots of French music, rolling around in bed, road trips and tears. I wish I lived in Paris right now. I think Paris could tolerate my feelings.

Southern California feels far too inadequate.

EVEN WHEN I HAVE ELECTRICITY,
I PREFER A CANDLELIT SHOWER.

> no noise and warm water
> no   make that hot water
> hot water and candles
>   dripping to the floor and
>   telling me to rest and to
> remember

ASK FIRST AND SHARE SECOND

Arvin is a little Indian boy who lives in my neighborhood. He stops by my office nearly every day with his sister. He is one of those boys who is terribly handsome and terribly messy and his pants legs are almost six inches too short and four times out of the week his shirt is on backward. Even when you tell Arvin his shirt is on backward, he seems okay with it. He is focused on bigger issues like passing his first grade congressional quiz and getting as much candy as he can from the offices around me. He's mastered the art of pacing himself. One office today, another on Thursday. Never letting any one office see him too many times. I don't have candy so Arvin comes to see me daily.

Without a doubt, my friend with pants two sizes too small launches into the story of his day. After perhaps five minutes, he takes a breath and starts on the second half of the story. I sit. I sit some more and then I ask him if he has a question for me.

Nope. As he looks around the room, impatiently, waiting for me to finish with my inquiry so he can get back to talking about him and his day. *Are you sure, Arvin? Are you sure you don't have a question for me?*

Noooooope. Nothing clearer could have come out of his mouth. He might be six but he's a smart ass.

I proceed to tell him how a gentleman asks a lady about her day, how a gentleman will ask questions and show concern for the person in front of him before discussing his story.

First of all, what? What am I supposed to ask? He says really disgruntled, head flat on my desk, arms sprawled and itching to walk out of my office with boredom. Arvin adds "first of all" to the beginning of as many sentences as possible. I think we have the same cowlick, Arvin and I. He has a piece of hair that sticks straight up just like me. I don't think he cares about that either.

Arvin, simply ask, 'How was your day?'

With all of the emphasis on the wrong word and with his eyes rolling to show his extreme displeasure at this new lesson, he tries it: *HOW was your day?* This isn't just six-year-old little Indian boys. Noooooope, it isn't. Our gut tendency is to talk about our day first and then, if the person in front of us is lucky, we might ask about her.

Poor little Arvin. He's just a boy. And adorable at that. And brilliant already, honestly. Unfortunately, he showed up in my office which was candy-less, so instead of chocolate he is getting life lessons.

I won't be to blame for any of his cavities. I might be to blame for him becoming a diplomat. And for that, I'd be quite honored.

Arvin came into my office Tuesday, sat down, asked, *HOW was your day?* with complete disinterest but at least he asked and said, *Did you know you won't die if you eat meat and you're a vegetarian? Pepperoni pizza is really good.*

Pepperoni pizza is good, Arvin. And, first of all, your shirt is on backward.

come home

I WAS LOST BUT NOW I'M FOUND.
I WAS ONLY A STREET AWAY.

DON'T ASK FOR PAIN

My friend E is a reporter and has decided to get tasered for his next story. Brilliant. He hasn't found a police department willing to do it yet although I'm sure there are plenty of cops "off the record" that would oblige. It's not that E is the sort of guy you want to tase but when someone asks for something like that, you say yes.

And, if they do find a department willing to do it, I hope they go full force and knock him on his ass. I don't mean to be cruel but why would you ask for pain of this sort? My seizures happen strictly at night and I'm really grateful for that. Some people, many people, most people don't have a clue when their seizures are going to hit and that's like walking around with someone holding a taser behind you but never knowing when they are going to press the button and not knowing if they are going to press it at full strength, mid, light, and aim at your head, heart or maybe just shoot up one leg.

That's sort of how a seizure can feel. You can walk around or sleep and everything seems completely normal and within mere seconds, there's this drop as if your body becomes cement and the worst part is the electrical storm happening in your brain.

Have you ever been tasered? Ever been electrocuted? I'm telling you, E is making the wrong decision. I cannot wait to watch. It's really going to hurt.

The difference with tasing and a seizure, during a seizure you don't know when it's going to end and you don't know sometimes if it's going to end with you ending. That's both the terrible and the beautiful part. It didn't used to be. I was in such pain that I would scream in agony not knowing what was happening to my body. As I got older, as the pre middle ageness set in, I stopped screaming.

The screaming wasn't helping and was tiring me out. Now, when a seizure comes, I roll with it, and at times, not knowing if I will ever catch my breath, there's this place of peace with God I'll rest in where I'll open my arms and say okay. Okay to going home. Okay to dying. Okay to not breathing again. Okay to being done with this part of my life. And okay to moving onto the next part of my life. The after party. I am an event planner.

I do hope the night it happens if it does happen that way I'm wearing the really good lingerie. Get some photos, won't you?

E, I'd think twice about the tasing. It hurts being electrocuted and having your body do things you don't ask it to do. It's not pleasant when your brain feels like it's cooking alive and you want it to end. Still, if you're going to do it, text me. I kinda can't wait. I might sell T-shirts.

THE PEOPLE THAT CHECK ON YOU POST-EARTHQUAKE
GET TO SPEAK AT YOUR FUNERAL.

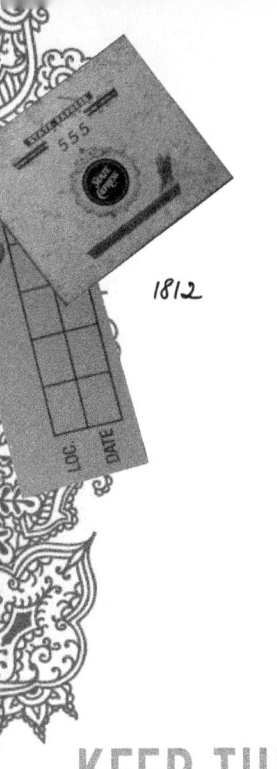

KEEP THINGS

Although I have great compassion for you hoarders, this is not for you. You don't need to keep things, you need to get rid of things. I'm talking to the rest of you. And I'm talking about pockets.

I love pockets. I bought this beautiful, sweet charcoal grey cashmere light as air Theory sweater the other day. I love sweaters almost to the point of illness and have particular fondness for The Cardigan. This one not only is a cardigan but has the best detailing and as I was out walking around the other day noticed it had two little pockets that were practically hidden. I noticed because I had been wearing the sweater inside out for two hours. Not good.

One on the left and one on the right. With zippers. So sweet. I love pockets and I love things that hold things. And things that don't let go of things.

Pockets are built for holding and for keeping and for not letting go. They say stay when things without pockets say *Tough Luck, Sunshine*. My mom had this book of writings and poetry she left us and I pull it out to read on the days when I need something in my pocket.

She has this one poem she wrote about my little brother and her at the beach. It's Brown Bear Summer and how she wishes to tuck the whole summer away in her pocket. I must have learned it from her in some place I don't remember but do remember when I reach my hand into a place where I need to keep things. Things like little cards from sweet hotels full of salty kisses and long goodbyes. Things like tickets to see places far away. Things like words and poems. And things you can't really physically tuck away but are the best things to keep in your pocket. Memories and sounds and smells and promises.

Those are my favorites. No, I don't need some large room to store all the things my heart wants to remember but I do need a small place to make sure they stay in and don't stay out. And a sweet little zipper would be lovely.

IT'S IMMATURE TO WISH A COUNTRY ILL.

WALLS ARE GOOD

On major holidays not including National Donut Day but things like New Year's Eve and such I like to head to Downtown L.A. for one reason. Walls. One wall in particular.

Parking underground is really light on these days. Most people are with someone but I have a desperate need for alone, not lonely, but Alone Time at least for a couple hours. I go up the red elevator and feel like I've come home. It's just to the right in that building over there and I'm almost there although I know rushing would make me look So Not L.A. so I'm going to take my time like I don't have to be in front of this piece now. I do have to be in front of this piece now.

It's not a wall, really, it's these two large steel brownish bands by Richard Serra at Los Angeles County Museum of Art that you can walk through but I don't want to walk through them and hardly ever do. I find my bench and set my purse down on the left realizing as I do I'm getting terribly set in my pre middle age ways but don't really give a damn. Leaning back and feeling the cool of the glass against me, I rest and look at my wall.

I need to look at a wall when I have walls in my life. Don't tell anybody. I talk at the wall. Not in some Zen way. I don't think the wall is going to answer me but I do think if I can throw my heart and my head and my worries and get them all out of the intense, dark place they are in and visually throw them on that space it helps.

And it does. I sit there and speak all my concerns and one by one all the questions and fears come to me and I write them down or sometimes text them to myself. There's no power in the wall so don't race to it looking for a tear or image of the Virgin Mary. There's power in admitting you have walls and not being afraid of them and talking through rather than walking around them.

This band, this wall is an art piece, but your walls are not. They are not to be mused over and adored and chatted about. Address them. They sit heavy in your room and heavy in your relationships filling up the whole space begging you to converse and act and make some changes.

You can sit on my bench if you'd like.

WILL'S SICK EGYPTIAN HUMOR INCLUDES TEXTING TO
SEE WHAT MOVIE I'M AT THEN TEXTING ME THE ENDING.

SET PARROTAL BOUNDARIES

I have this beautiful office in Downtown Orange County, California. Think The Wedding Planner meets The OC but without electricity and with McDonald's.

So, I'm sitting in my office and in walks this incredibly distraught woman holding...a parrot. A baby one. She sits down and looks to be in shock and then she asks for a box to put the parrot in. Seems she was walking over by the park and found the bird and wants to care for it until she finds its owner.

Very sweet I say and wish her well and find the best baby parrot holding box I can find. She gets ready to leave and has this pained look on her face. *Do you know what I should feed it? I don't. Do you know what I should do if no one claims it? I don't. I'm sorry.*

She continues to walk out my front door going slower and slower and almost makes it all the way past the door frame then turns. *I don't think I can care for this bird.* In code and with heavy, almost-spilling tears she's saying I want you to care for this bird.

As much as I appreciate animals and baby ones at that, this is your little sweet adventure, my dear sweet baby parrot holding friend. And you chose to pick it up and involve yourself but I didn't. I involve myself in lots of other non-parrot like things that take up much of my time, which is why I choose to say no to this.

No. It's a hard word for us pre middle agers to say. Men and women. We are fond of The Yes and delivering on things and being the hero and people saying how much we can accomplish and …I'm exhausted just thinking of your inbox with all your yeses. No. Not so easy to say no when people expect much out of us and think the world of us and see talent in us. And no seems to be such a small word, something that should roll off the tongue but it doesn't. No. It doesn't.

It takes effort to tell people you will not take their baby parrot and find its mother. It takes effort to set boundaries all around your pre middle age life. It takes effort to say no when our heart and brain and guts and, most important, pride are yearning to say yes. Practice. Start with parrots if that helps.

THE HOMELESS ARE YOU AND ME BUT WITH BETTER MANNERS.
what to keep and what to
give and then

give some more

BE AN EXPERT AT YOU

Had a dream the other night. There was very delicate heart surgery happening and I was watching from a distance. A surgeon was called in to perform the work and someone else came rushing in. It was an eyeball surgeon. Shh. That's what he was called in my dream, so that's what we're going to call him.

The eyeball surgeon was not only skilled at performing surgery on eyeballs but was world renowned for eyeball repair. If you needed your eyeball fixed, he was the man to call. He should practically have a cape with a big E on the back of it. For eyeball.

This, this was heart surgery though, and I was the one that had to call out and say to the team the news no one seemed to realize: *He's an eyeball surgeon. The cardiac guy needs to do this job!*

You are amazing at what you are amazing at. You really would be horrendous at heart surgery, though, without the proper training. And in like manner, it is our nature to want to puff our career chests and take on tasks and assignments either well beyond our ability or that someone else has earned the right to do. If you want to go work in cardiac medicine, by all means, train for it, eyeball doctor, but please don't nudge your way into someone else's job because you're overeager.

I see this all the time and have been this so many times. Admitting this is a little hard especially for go-getter types like me. We think we can do everything. And sure, maybe there are many things I can do really well, but I'd like to do a couple things amazingly well. I'd prefer to be a superstar rather than running to every fire trying to prove to people I can perform surgery, change tires and fix global warming. I mean I can but ….

Dr. Eyeball Fixer Man and all of you who impatiently want to do something other than the thing you are doing, continue. Continue to work with excellence. Do your thing and do it well. In time, it will pay off and then if you want to do something else you can go do that. You will never, ever succeed by taking someone else's surgery, even in my dream.

LOCKED DOORS ARE LOCKED FOR A REASON.

IT'S CLEARER UP HERE, NO HERE

Bursting with love for all things Joan Mitchell. You don't have to be an art fan. And I would call myself a very immature one, really. Remember, I like simple but when something grabs my heart or makes me full of passion or angst, I cannot help but respond to it. Joan Mitchell's art does that to me.

Renoir? Sometimes.

She was an Abstract Expressionist, and the first time I saw her work was in Los Angeles. It was one of those days when I was museum and creative roaming and trying the best I could to figure out how to design a gala I was going to be throwing. Seeing color and light and design helps me put together color and light and design. I start looking at the creative places and I always start where my mom took me as a child.

L.A. and her museums.

I was on the second floor heading toward the back and made a left and there it was. Her painting took, and to this day, takes my breath away. I get excited just telling you about it. I do hope you see it one day. It's full of the most brilliant color which goes against everything my mother taught me. *Stay with earth tones and keep your makeup palette neutral and when all else fails...taupe.* My insides were screaming for Mitchell's colors. I was in love.

I sat down to watch and feel the painting and let people stand in front of it and tilted to the right so I could peer around them and then leaned to the left to peer around the other way. I couldn't take my eyes off it. Something about it stood out more than so many other beautiful works of art in the same lovely room. I had my back to Rothko for God's sake.

And I realized. The bottom of her work is very dark and chaotic. I wonder what was happening as she painted that portion and as she heads towards the middle of the work it gets less and less so. Then, you near the top and everything shifts. There's an air and a calm and a peace and sweetness and space about the lines and movement. It's as if all her time and thoughts opened up. It's me.

When things are dark in my life, they are really dark and the chaos is really chaotic and I have to press myself to move above it and to go higher and trust that things are better above than below. When I'm reaching for something more rather than wallowing in what is lost or what feels mussed, I am well. I may not be whole. I might be broken and bloodied and bruised from a battle but I'm well. It's the reaching that I need to do because I'm damn sure not able to do this on my own and need the bigness of God to do it for me and with me.

It gets clearer that way. There's more space that way. Less chaotic that way.

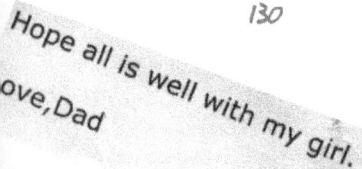

Hope all is well with my girl. Love, Dad

I REALLY SHOULD TALK TO MY THERAPIST ABOUT THIS.
I REALLY SHOULD FIND A THERAPIST.

YOU ARE NOT A COUGAR

Fuming, absolutely fuming almost to the point of becoming a car horn honker and you know that's a really dark place for me. Time came out with an article, "The Science of Cougar Sex." Now, I'm all for women and sexuality. What I'm not for, what I'm absolutely against is this term. I've been over it since it came out. Cougar.

I'm not an animal. You calling me one doesn't make me one. I'm a woman. Maybe I'm an age that makes you uncomfortable. I don't care. Maybe my sexuality bothers you a bit. You don't seem to mind when you have your hand on my ass. Maybe it's my strong personality. In business, you need it when I negotiate deals you are afraid to touch. I'm not sure which part of me being a woman makes me like an animal to you but in any case, I'm not. I'm not an animal.

C is for many other things

And you are not. You, you beautiful women. You pre middle age and middle age women that are just starting to see wrinkles in places you never saw them and fear smiling for forming more around your eyes. Smile. And maybe you looked down and there is gray hair in places that just makes you want to vomit. You are still beautiful.

It doesn't mean you have to start dating 22 year olds and paying for their college education or buying their meals. It doesn't mean men your age won't date you because of some ridiculous stigma the media has tried to place on you.

You are lovely and sweet and sometimes, yes, very moody but very talented and you've worked hard to earn a good living. Nothing about you is animalistic. You don't have to go to those bars and pick up those guys.

And if you are playing that role, the cougar role and falling into that stereotype, I think you should know people are laughing at you. I don't say it to hurt your feelings but to awaken you. I hear the men talk and whisper to each other as they spot you in your too short skirt and over teased hair and plastered face and well, plastered self. *Cougar at 2 o'clock.* I look over and you are there and it hurts my heart that you don't know a young man is about to take advantage of you, sleep with you and more than likely try to use you for what money he hopes you have. Be the better you, you are. I know you are lonely but you are not alone. There's a you to get back to and the sooner you fish your brain out of your Louis Vuitton, the sooner you'll find love. The real kind. The kind that whispers in your ear rather than behind your back.

I ONLY USE THE FAKE BOOBS ON REALLY IMPORTANT DAYS. I ALWAYS FESS UP TO THEM.

Cole's Top 12 Lessons of 2009

12. Don't let your car insurance expire. No, really. Don't. I need a ride
11. Take time to listen to Ruth at the drive thru's jaw surgery saga. Ruth matters. People matter. Their little details matter.
10. People are more important than the party.
9. What you are looking for is right here, no there. I mean it's in front of you.
8. Kissing good looking men in good looking bars is, yep, still fun.
7. A text relationship is not a relationship.
6. Mentor someone. Be generous with your gorgeous brain.
5. Let compliments flow faster than eye rolls.
4. Buy someone coffee for no reason other than they are an a✕✕.
3. Gain a proper sense of emergency. Things that are not? Balloon columns. Catching green lights. Coffee.
2. Say sorries. Say I'm wrongs. Say you're rights.
1. When you see the person with the look that says, 'don't #$%'n talk to me' #$%'n talk to them.

HANDLE WITH CARE

You've seen "A Christmas Story," haven't you? If not, rent it in some non-December month. That's when, Miss Chloe and I like to listen to Christmas carols. Sure, you might walk into our office and think we've lost it but bringing in the cheer in the middle of a heat wave works.

A Christmas Story. It's the dead of summer right now and I was taking one of those naps where you coma just a tad. The thought of not waking up begins to sound like a fabulous option. I love naps like that. And in the midst my nap, I dream of the box. You know, the one in "A Christmas Story." Fragile. The dad wins a prize from some contest. It shows up at the door and it's tilted to the side when it should be upright, is marked fragile and has a leg lamp inside.

That's me tonight. Tilted to the side when I need someone to lift me upright because everything marked on the side of me says FRAGILE. And no one seems to see the writing. So, it lays there, tilted and in it is a leg, not two, which is really what I need right now to run this race at full speed, but one. Sure, in real life, I have both my legs about me and am very grateful for that when some are limited to less. In the dream, one leg. And in the box, one leg. And in my life and especially this evening, feeling very one legged. Limited in my ability to finish this race.

The dad in "A Christmas Story" doesn't see one leg as less than. In fact, he digs it and places the lamp covered in one-legged fishnets in the middle of the living room for all the neighbors to see. Not a thought runs through his head that there is a thing missing from this lamp or from this box.

Maybe there isn't from me either. Maybe I'm supposed to get knocked on my side on occasion and maybe even when all signs point to FRAGILE even then maybe people will be rough with me. And, perhaps what feels like a limitation, this feeling of only having one leg about me, is really something to light up and put in the middle of the living room for the whole neighborhood to see.

Hi neighbors. It's Cole. I'm flawed and running a bit slow in the race. But I will finish. Handle with care please.

I WISH TODAY WAS NATIONAL DONUT DAY.

PUT UP THE CANVAS

I don't want you to know this since anytime I'm not good at something I like to tuck it away until I am a Jedi Master. I think I'm being encouraged to step outside of that but this is a hard one for me. I imagined myself painting today and on the arm of the canvas, the canvas having an arm since I was the artist and could do what I wished, I left my name. I've never signed my name to a canvas since I've never had the nerve to touch one.

My grandmother was the artist and my mother sketched and I never dreamed I would put hand to paint. I figured if you can't be a Joan Mitchell then stay home.

I'm wrong. I crave almost every day to buy a canvas and paint. I don't know what the hell I'm doing but I still want to do it. It's the same with every other pursuit in my life. I've gone jumping off the cliff appearing completely brave, but that was only after years of fear sitting on the edge.

I'm weary of waiting in the sidelines with paint. I don't need masterpieces but I do need to try. Trying is what my pre middle age years are about. I've risked much in my trying but my tries have paid off. Great love and great friendships and great learnings and great experiences and great adventures.

I'm going to buy a canvas. I suppose I'll need some paint. Perhaps a brush or two will help. Beyond that, I don't really know what's next but I'm going to paint and I'll definitely sign my name on the side of the canvas, on the arm of the canvas because that's where I saw it in and that's where it will be.

RUTH AT MCDONALD'S: NEVER SAID, YOU MARRIED?
ME: NOPE. I WAS.
RUTH: SMART WOMAN.

YOUR TELL IS YOUR TELL

Was driving through McDonald's the other day. I know. I do it far more often than a pre middle age woman should but occasionally I like a Diet Coke and a chocolate chip cookie. Ruth always asks *Just one today, Cole?* It's been one cookie at the drive thru for over a year but every time she says that I know the cookies have to stop. One day.

For now, I get to visit with Ruth. Most of our visits are quick as they should be when she has fewer than 30 seconds to take my order, cash and hand back change. We sometimes break the rule. Shh, don't let her McDonald's franchise owner know.

I know much about Ruth this way. She's a grandma and has this long gray braid that I'm sure takes so much time to unfurl and wash. She smokes and has a crackly smoker voice and crackly smoker teeth. And her smile is the smile of someone that knows the dirty jokes. She doesn't share them with me.

See, Ruth is on the headset and I don't think McDonald's wants her asking *Would you like to try our new McCafe and did you hear the one about the....?*

Yes, Ruth's teeth and her crackliness let off many clues to her story. I do know she has a daughter named Carrie and her and her son-in-law fight all the time. And her other daughter lives back east and had the chubbiest, most angelic little baby. I wonder if that's what Ruth looked like when she was a baby and had fresh, ungray hair and all her teeth and not a crackly laugh of an older woman who smoked but maybe a young giggle of a child loved.

Ruth sighs quite a bit lately. It's her tell. I've learned not to rush through window number two because if Ruth sighs she has something she needs to get off her chest. She could simply tell me, *Cole, I need to tell you about my day. Would you listen?*

I would listen. I wouldn't hesitate to listen. I would park my car and wait for her break and listen. Ruth doesn't do that though. She sighs and the heavier the sighs the worse the news. A sigh that causes her chest to raise more than two inches in the air is rather significant news.

I put the car in neutral for those sighs,

You can skip the tell and tell instead. People will listen to you. The eye rolls and the sighs and the prefacing and the tantrums are really not needed. You can tell.

I'll have a number five with a Diet Coke. It was Monday morning and by a Christmas Miracle in the middle of the summer I made it to McDonald's before 10:30 a.m. It was 10:29 a.m.

Is that you, Cole? Ruth knows my car and my rentals and likes the Prius almost as much as me. I get to her window and as she takes my change a heavy *Please Ask Me What's Wrong Sigh* comes off her chest.

Ruth, are you okay? Carrie kicked me out of the house because of that damn husband of hers and my car broke down and luckily I have one sister that has money and I made it to Pep Boys and the repair was only $129.24 and she paid it for me and I had to move to Garden Grove and I'm living with this *family. I haven't seen my grandbaby yet but they are coming out soon. Do you want to see her new picture?*

Cannot wait until Ruth feels comfortable telling without the introductory sigh but for now, I'll watch for her tell.

APPLAUD, DON'T MOCK THE BRAVERY OF BROKEN ENGLISH.

your language is rough and
  abrupt and harsh to someone else but
to me it is fluid and lovely and
reminds me of

  peeled oranges on paper towels.

YOU ARE PART NOT THE WHOLE

My father used to fume at me when I was little. We would walk in crowded spaces, malls, outdoor shopping centers and I would take my purse with its long handle and swing it. Not only swinging but get as much momentum in the swing as possible. It felt good on my arm, that tension and pull and my brain wasn't really thinking of anything other than how fast and hard I could get the purse to turn into a living energy source.

Turns out I was Green long before the rest of you.

Dad would tell me to stop and for a moment I would and my purse would smack against my thigh. And not thinking, in the midst of another crowd or in that very same spot without even two minutes from the last time he told me to stop, I would start again. Revving the purse and slowly getting enough tension in it to whip it in the air.

You're going to hit someone and they are going to say something to you and I'm really going to say something to you. My dad never laid a hand on me but that phrase alone sure made it sound like he could. I'd put the purse down again. Until I started. Again.

It's the nature of immaturity to be so wrapped up in self that I couldn't possibly think my swinging purse could injure someone. The thought didn't even cross my childish mind. How could it? I wasn't wired to think outside of me, my little brain or doing exactly what I wanted to do at the exact moment I wanted to do it.

Now, don't get me wrong, I was one of those children with a heavy compassionate heart for the hurting and the lonely and the person without food, clothing or shelter. But that didn't deter me from going deep inside my head many times a day and thinking of nothing other than me.

It's natural. It's the course of child to do that. And ideally as we age the need to think of self only or self first gets less and less. And the want to think of the hurting and the lonely and the person without food, clothing or shelter gets more and more. The scary thing is when it doesn't and you are pre middle age. Have you seen that? Those people that walk into a bank and throw a fit because something is wrong with their deposit. Or maybe at a restaurant because their steak isn't cooked exactly right.

They are swinging their purse in the air without a thought for the tens and hundreds around them that are living, too. Maybe in the middle of your restaurant rant, you don't realize that your server is in the middle of a divorce or the hostess just got beat by her boyfriend. Or maybe the bank manager's dad is dying of cancer and he just got the news or stopped by hospice to see him one last time.

You're swinging your purse, you grown adult. And it's hitting people and the world is about more than you. And someone is going to get hit by it and hurt by it.

You are part of a whole, like me. And as we age, how beautiful to know that when we walk into a space, the space is about more than us. Make room for people. Don't swing so hard.

SELIM FROM THE CORNER MARKET SPENT TONIGHT TELLING ME HOW HE TALKS TO AN EMPTY PASSENGER SEAT. HE'S STILL IN LOVE WITH THE WOMAN

WHO USED TO SIT THERE.

LEARN THE STEPS TO LEAD

There was a dance recital last night in my sleep. I sleep in color and in sound. And sometimes in tutus. Last night was one of those nights.

I grew up taking lessons of all sorts: swim from Mrs. Boerlin and flute from Ms. Helm and Spanish from Ms. Rodriguez who would come to the house while I was recovering from an extended time of illness during my teenage years. Every teacher expected me to have practiced during the week. Being a master procrastinator, I waited 'til 30 minutes before their arrival or before session started and lessoned up.

Sometimes it worked. Sometimes it didn't.

One of the instructors from my youth was The Burgundy Ballerina. She was my first real dance instructor after going to numerous classes here and there. The Burgundy Ballerina launched her business out of her garage. She had the barre and mirrors and ballerinas that were tall and talented and young and absentminded. I was young and absentminded.

And she always, always wore burgundy which really wasn't, and to this day, isn't a favorite color of mine but I admire her commitment to her brand.

The Burgundy Ballerina taught us routines for practice and routines for recitals and always, always knew all the steps. She would stand in front with what looked to me like a wand and direct. We learned to follow her lead and eventually to remember her instruction.

And there were times when, at recitals, the nerves of a young, very young absentminded dancer would take hold and The Burgundy Ballerina would come on stage to a row full of frightened tutus. Tutus not sure what to do next and stumbling around and next to each other looking for instruction and help. Our instructor, knowing the steps, would lead us back into calm and one by one, pink tutus and black leotards and light pink tights and little buns would float in unison.

To lead, you need to know the steps. In my multicolored sleep, I was standing in front of a row of girls, like these sweet little ones and they were confused and I didn't know the steps. It wasn't my place to lead if I hadn't taken the time to learn the routine.

To lead you need to know the steps and the routine and the music and the people performing and all the details. They are watching your feet for guidance and your hands for direction and your face for assurance.

To lead you need to know the steps. It's okay if you don't. Someone else can step in and lead until you do, but don't lead the routine if you don't. You'll only confuse the dancers.

And most of all, most important of all, piss off the parents.

first position

I'M INTIMIDATED BY SOME MUSIC AND SOME ART AND SOME LECTURES.

I GO ANYWAY.

go and see and do and
then experience and see some more and
feel and maybe hear or perhaps touch and
then taste something
that you haven't before

SHE NEEDS IT MORE THAN YOU

His name is Jack. I wasn't sure if that was his name until yesterday but that is, in fact, his name. He's dark gray and rather small and covered in fur and has a price tag on his right ear which I took off just before handing him over to Fickle Mia. She quickly fell for him. Fickle Mia and I are alike is so very many ways.

   Jack, the stuffed animal hippo, was sitting on a shelf in Toys R Us Friday night. Not a very exciting place to spend a Friday night, but there is the rare occasion when I step foot inside a toy store. I grabbed a cart, put my bag inside and mere minutes later, walking down the left side aisle, spotted Jack. He was rather alone. And it was clearer to me than anything else could be clear that the only place he belonged was in my cart. Sure, I could have thrown him in the basket like any other toy as if he was any other sort of stuffed animal but I took an instant liking to Jack. I put him in the baby seat, that front one, what do you parents call it? The one where you bring your own sanitized baby seat protector cover thing and it probably has a drink holder for your "soda" as well.

I set him there and, to avoid looking like I was straight headed for Crazy Land, which is around the corner, I avoided talking to Jack. Well, I whispered to him. In my heart.

Out of the toy store and into the car and Jack made it into the back seat, which is where you put the precious things, and there he stayed until movie night. And that's when I saw Fickle Mia. She came bursting toward me with her brother and her dad and her outdoor movie food and outdoor movie blankets and outdoor movie ringleted curls. They found their spot, burrowed in like my non-pretty wrinkles do and waited for the movie to begin.

And I felt an urge to go get Jack. See, I wanted to keep him and hand him off at times to Miss Chloe for story time with at Starbucks but I looked a Fickle Mia and knew, just knew the way you know, that Jack belonged with her. I grabbed him and took him to her and asked her if she would watch him for me during the movie.

Her little 6-year-old fingers grabbed him as hard as they did gentle. She didn't set him down once. I knew he was in good hands. And after the movie, I walked up to her and her eyes looked as if I was going to take away her very beating heart. Still, she was willing to let Jack the Hippo go.

Mia, would you do me a favor? Would you keep Jack and would you take care of him and would you read to him because I think he really likes books?

Mia looked at me with the chocolatiest eyes and shouted, Y*es!* Running to tell her dad that she was the proud owner of a dark gray, stuffed, book-loving hippo, she suddenly turned to me with tears in her eyes and said, *Cole, aren't you going to be sad to let him go?* Wiping tears from my own eyes I assured her I would be fine.

I am going to be fine, right?

If you find yourself in the giving place and there is a person that will light up from your smallest gesture. Then do it, gesture. Give. Take what you have and make it someone else's have. Fickle Mia has assured me that she is showing Jack the Hippo *where the bathroom is tonight and he's sleeping with me and I'm putting a T-shirt on him.*

I didn't know hippos wore T-shirts but I have much to learn in my late 30s.

IT ONLY TOOK THREE DAYS TO BRIGHTEN THE DASHBOARD.
MY RENTAL SKILLS ARE ACCELERATING.

NAPS HELP

I told you I don't believe in those fancy matchboxes. Well, it's not that I don't believe in them but I don't think women in Orange County should blare their horns at me as they race to stores to get them for their precious little parties.

Hold off judgment when I go get them for my precious little party because everything I judge I become.

Matchboxes. This one is different from those. It is from Rogers Gardens, you know, with the ladies in the safest shades of taupe and this matchbox was one of a lovely stack in the front of the store off to the right. I adore lovely stacks of things that I find as I walk off to the right and off to the left. I told you. This wasn't just any matchbox.

There's a mouse inside. He has a blanket, well, three really, so he has some options and there's even a pillow with sweet little dots on it so that he doesn't get bored with the plainness of it all.

There's nothing plain about this matchbox. This matchbox is a bed. And this mouse is resting inside, napping, really.

Nap being one of my all-time favorite things to do.

Rest. If you haven't learned the art of resting by now, learn it. Find your matchbox, all decorated in soft circus shades and colors to delight your eyes. Get your softest blankets and, if you don't have them, go and buy them. Find the pillow that makes you sigh a sigh of relief when your face touches it. And tuck away every once in a while and rest.

You're not too old for naps. You're not too powerful for them either. And running yourself into the ground trying to show everyone how you can do 14 hours of work in three hours isn't really helping anyone.

Seriously. Haven't you seen Cinderella? Mice know things.

ART IS WORTH TRAFFIC.
YOU ARE WORTH TRAFFIC.

DON'T CATCH PEOPLE

The 405 freeway is moving along just fine. Sting is shouting to Roxanne and reminding her to put out her red light, which is always a good reminder and I see it. A California Highway Patrol cruiser tucked behind a tree just waiting to catch someone running one of those incoming carpool lights. Oh, I don't know what those are called either. 'Cause they don't have traffic lights on freeways, but you know the ones as you come onto the freeway. Those. And he's sitting there and waiting to nab a person. It's not like they are driving 90 on the freeway or drunk or texting and driving or even just an all-around terribly slow driver like me. No. This CHP has a goal and he wants to catch you getting onto the freeway and running that red.

I can almost see his finger pointing at you now saying, *Aha!*

It's like us and people. We have that tendency to want to catch them screwing up and then calling it out in really big, obvious ways and making a scene about it. I did it today. The IT Help Desk really blew a ticket request I needed assistance with and rather than working through it with them I made a point of pointing out their screw-up. Why? Because it's our nature to want to say you blew it and you suck and I don't.

But I do. That's the problem.

I hate that about me. I hated it today. It's so easy for me to tear someone down rather than build them up and I'm a good builder upper, but today and that moment got the better of me. I was the cop waiting for you to run that red light and couldn't wait to point my finger and call you out.

I'm sorry about that. Robert. At the IT Help Desk. Ext. 2349.

I'd like to be nicer than that. Kinder than that. Sweeter than that, not in the fake way but in the real, real way where I feel it in my heart. I'd like to put my finger down and when you screw up realize it's half as many times as I do.

I use to scream aha. Now I say it with snark and a raised brow. It's still just as mean. I'm going to have to phone Robert tomorrow and apologize.

I DON'T WANT TO BE AN ADULT TODAY.

                              i miss playing bride on
                              rio lempa drive
                                         and backyard carnivals
                 and
                 jeans full of caked mud
                 from sliding down hills with
                 boys

168 23304 and 22

YOUR WORDS COUNT

My assistant is great. I'll rant and rave in the very pre middle age way I do when a very long work day gets to me and I've made the fourth change to a creative that shouldn't require changes at all. My head laying on the desk in a very dramatic style tells the world I am overworked and ready for the day to end. It's my tell.

Miss Chloe throws out a one-liner under her breath like *time for dinner* or when I'm jealous over someone throwing an amazing party in L.A. with 10 times the budget I have and 10 times the press I have she says *'Eff LA*. She's good like that. To my 20 words she's got two and maybe even one.

She takes my longs and makes them short and they work and we work and it works. At times I wonder if all my words and my almost middle ageness annoy her the way people older than me used to annoy me. They talked so much and had so much to say and I wanted to get on with my day and could you please simply shut it?

Now, I'm the talker and the one with the words and come across so many of you with words of your own and it grieves me when you worry that you have too much to say as you start to rush to finish. Don't ever rush to finish your words with me and when I ask you how you are, answer me because I'm really asking I'm not asking in the Walking Around The Corner To Go Do Something Else way.

I want to hear your words. I'm sorry for all the times and years someone rushed you. So very sorry for the years you lost in turning your life into bullet points and sound bites feeling as if you had five minutes or 15 seconds to run down the deep furrowed worries of your heart and your brain and your soul. Your words matter. The big ones and the small ones and the ones you say loud and the ones you say soft and especially the ones you say gasping for breath through muffled tears. You don't have to muffle them. Well, you're going to make a scene, but I'm okay with scenes.

I had coffee. Oh, I had de-caf with a woman the other day and she emailed me a sweet follow-up along with a hand-written note. Both included her apology for taking up my time. She is a generation past me and for some odd, some very sad reason felt her words didn't hold enough weight for our brief one-hour conversation. I wanted more. More of her time. More of her knowledge. More of the grace she had and I lacked. More of her smarts to my stupid. I could have spent an afternoon with her and her words.

As we age, we have more to say but are more hesitant to say it. Yes, I suppose there's wisdom to choosing words carefully. Still, when you are with me, I want to hear it all. I have time. And your words count. To me they do.

IT'S HERE

You're taunting me, 40 and 50 and all the way up to 90. I see you on the horizon and you dare me to live you out with dignity and grace and respect rather than going down in a ball of flames.

I'm up to the challenge. I've got it in me. I think there's a few solid brain cells left up here to take you on. I was dreaming the other night, as I'm ought to do, and thought of a writer I've followed with great affection. He has since passed but made a point of gathering his thoughts, his thoughts just for him on the chance he lost all of his marbles one day. Then, the writings would be a space and place for him to look back and remember what he knew and know it somewhere deep once again.

These are my lessons. I'm not sure how long I'll have all my marbles but as long as there's at least one yellow one rolling around in my bag, I'll share it with you. And before I head out 20 more pre middle age tips for the road. These are on me. Thought you'd like the sound of 20 one last time.

1. French music helps everything.
2. Don't marry someone you don't love to kiss.
3. Say good evening and good day. Bring back civility.
4. If someone smells lovely, tell them.
5. Quiet is okay. So is space. Everything doesn't have to be filled.
6. Turn the bass down unless you're about to sign a record deal.
7. Tip the donut guy.
8. If you ask someone how they are, wait for their whole answer.
9. Be kind to their mean.
10. Give presents on your birthday one year in your life.
11. For three small seconds close your eyes and remember.
12. Odds are okay. Odds are even better. Odds are preferred.
13. Cry as needed. Repeat.
14. At a museum, you don't have to feel what they feel. Simply feel.
15. The thing you think of first upon rising is your greatest idol.
16. An adventure can be as slight as conversation. Have one.
17. A shower will help. So will a glass of water. So will a humidifier. So will a wet washcloth on the forehead. Think moist.
18. If the guy on the corner of State Street says the world is going to end on May 6, 2014, I'd at least mark the calendar.
19. Unless really lonely, taxi driver proposals of marriage should be taken with a grain of salt.
20. And always, always put your money on the longshot.

That's you, huh? A longshot. Wondering how this whole thing is going to turn out. Every day pre middle age is full of twists and turns and calls that come in the middle of the night making changes to your life that you didn't expect. I like when the calls are good calls. I'm sorry when they are calls that make you grieve.

You are a walker outer, my friend. I cannot wait to see how you walk out these next years and excited to see you grow into the adult you so want to be. Much love to you as we walk this out together. I promise not to stomp my feet too often.

ely to spend time with
and share words with you
even whole bunches of
ntences

ACKNOWLEDGMENTS

Thanks to Todd Harmonson, John and Chris Blue, Michelle Reines, Kelly Harmonson and Will Naguib. This would not be possible without you.

And to 213 Downtown LA, Cole's French Dip, Carli Huston, Shelly Romanosky and Amy Kaplan Photo for bringing The Pretty.

www.ingramcontent.com/pod-product-compliance
Lightning Source LLC
Chambersburg PA
CBHW051758040426
42446CB00007B/423